Someone had broken into the pharmacy and left it in ruins.

The Crime Scene

Items had been swept off the shelves and scattered all over the floor. Bottles and boxes of medicines had been ripped open, and drugs were missing. The cash register was open, too—and empty.

The Mystery

It was clearly a robbery. But how had the burglar gotten into and out of the store? The back door and windows were still locked from the inside.

In fact, besides the mess, the burglar had left no sign of his presence. There were no smashed windows. No broken locks. And no fingerprints!

Dusting for Prints

No prints?

Fingerprint specialists had dusted every inch of the crime scene. But so far, they hadn't found any unidentified prints anywhere.

The Question

How would detectives find enough evidence to point to a suspect? Why is it unlikely that a criminal could commit a crime and not leave any evidence behind?

Book Design: Red Herring Design/NYC **Photo Credits:** Photographs © 2012: Alamy Images: 34 (Sally & Richard Greenhill), 47 (Eric Nathan), 13 (Pablo Paul), 20 center bottom (Stock Take), 20 center top (vario images GmbH & Co.KG), 26 (A. T. Willett); AP Images: 15 (Chris Schneider), 40 top center (Toby Talbot); Armor Forensics: 42 5-A; Corbis Images: 42 3-C (Randy Faris), 42 2-A (Thom Lang), 42 1-A (Robert Llewellyn); DK Images: 30 center right, 40 bottom left; Courtesy of the FBI: 35; Getty Images: 10 (Tony Anderson), 2, 3 (Phil Walter); iStockphoto/Peter Kim: 44; JupiterImages/Laurent Hamels: 41 bottom; Media Bakery: back cover background, cover (Gary S. Chapman), back cover foreground (Steve Weisbauer), 16, 19, 20 top, 22, 25, 32; NEWSCOM/c51/ZUMA Press: 4, 5; Photo Researchers, NY: 14 right (Michael Donne), 8, 20 center (Mauro Fermariello), 14 left, 20 bottom (Philippe Psaila); PhotoEdit/Dana White: 42 2-B; Photolibrary/Creatas: 41 top; Red Herring: 24, 41 center left; Reprinted from "Prints and Impressions", Scholastic, Inc., 2003: 30 top right, 30 bottom right, 31; ShutterStock, Inc.: 29 screen (Kevin L. Chesson), 29 monitor (Kjolak), 36 (Philip Lange), 30 left (OLJ Studio), 37 (PzAxe); Sirchie Fingerprint Laboratories: 40 top left, 40 bottom right, 41 center right; Superstock, Inc./Exactostock: 1; Tennessee Bureau of Investigation: 28, 40 top right; TheChattanoogan.com/Dennis Norwood: 38; VEER/Digital Vision: 43 5-D; Visuals Unlimited/Dave Olson: 43 4-D.

Unless noted, images on page 42-43 are courtesy of Sirchie Fingerprint Laboratories or Red Herring.

Library of Congress Cataloging-in-Publication Data

Beres, D. B.
Sticky evidence : burglar caught on tape / D.B. Beres.
p. cm.
Includes bibliographical references and index.
ISBN-13 978-0-545-32803-6
ISBN-10 0-545-32803-9
1. Fingerprints—Juvenile literature. 2. Fingerprints—Identification—Juvenile literature.
3. Forensic sciences—Juvenile literature. 4. Criminal investigation—Juvenile literature. I. Title.
HV6074.B373 2011
363.25'8—dc22
2011005195

 Pages printed on 10% PCW recycled paper.

1 2 3 4 5 6 7 8 9 10   40   21 20 19 18 17 16 15 14 13 12

STICKY EVIDENCE

Burglar Caught on Tape

D. B. BERES

TABLE OF CONTENTS

1

Without a Trace

A drugstore robbery leaves a huge mess— and a lot of questions.

Bob Moranes got a terrible surprise when he arrived at work one Saturday morning.

Moranes was the owner of Gooch Pharmacy near Chattanooga, Tennessee. On the morning of October 15, 2005, he unlocked the store, as usual.

But when he walked into his drugstore, his heart jumped. The pharmacy was a mess. The shelves had been swept clean. Empty boxes and medicine bottles littered the floor. The cash register had been forced open, and all the money was gone. A lot of drugs were missing, too.

Moranes picked up the phone and called the police.

Not long after, the police fingerprint team arrived at the drugstore. These specialists prepared to process the scene and find any fingerprints that the burglar had left behind.

Missing Prints

Burglars often leave fingerprints all over a crime scene. Everyone's fingerprints are unique. No two people share the same pattern of fingerprints. That makes them great evidence for identifying people.

The fingerprint specialists dusted the cash register. But all the prints belonged to people who worked at the store.

They dusted all the empty medicine boxes and bottles that were out of place. No prints.

How had the burglar made such a mess of the pharmacy without leaving any prints?

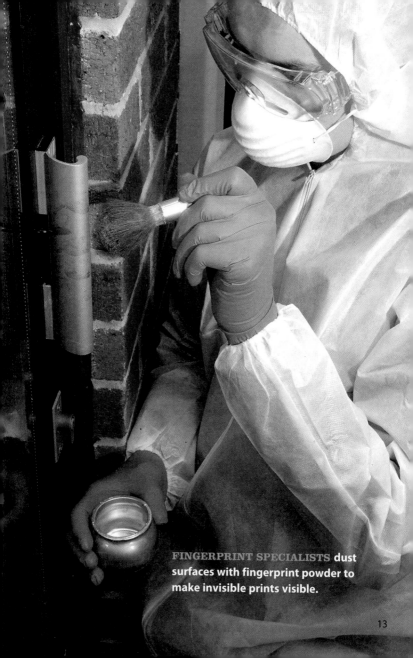

FINGERPRINT SPECIALISTS dust surfaces with fingerprint powder to make invisible prints visible.

Don't Forget to Dust

Here's what fingerprint specialists do at the crime scene.

1. Wait for the photographer.
Before anyone else touches the crime scene, a police photographer takes pictures. That way, there's a record of what the scene looked like before the investigation began.

2. Check out the crime scene.
Fingerprint specialists look for prints on anything the perp (short for perpetrator) might have touched, like doors, walls, counters, and furniture.

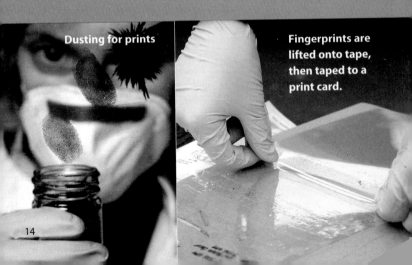

Dusting for prints

Fingerprints are lifted onto tape, then taped to a print card.

3. Dust for prints.
The specialists brush these surfaces with powder that sticks to the oil and sweat in fingerprints. This makes the prints more visible.

4. Document the evidence.
Specialists use something sticky, like tape, to capture a print. Then they stick the tape to a card. They note the date and place where the print was found. They may also photograph the print and scan it into a computer.

5. Gather other evidence.
Are there any weapons or tools at the scene? Specialists take them back to the lab and check them for prints, too.

6. Find a match.
If there's a suspect, specialists will compare the prints from the crime scene to the suspect's. If there's not a suspect, specialists can run the prints through IAFIS, a computer database that stores millions of prints.

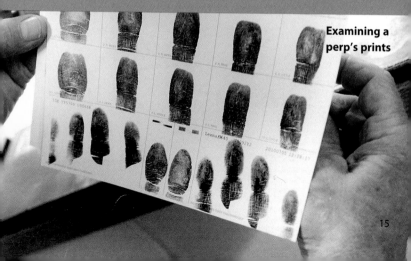

Examining a perp's prints

15

2

Secret Entrance

Can investigators figure out how the burglar broke into the store?

The absence of fingerprints wasn't the only mystery at the crime scene. Police also didn't understand how the thief had entered and exited the store. The back door and windows were still locked from the inside. So the thief must have found another way to get into the drugstore.

But what was it?

The police found a clue in the office at the back of

the store. The cover to a heating duct in the ceiling had been removed. (Ducts are passages that allow air to circulate through a building.) And a desk had been moved directly under the opening to the duct.

Where did the duct lead? The police traced it to the heating system on the roof of the building. Next to the heating system was an opening to the duct.

Dropping In

The police developed a theory about how the burglar had entered and exited the store. The burglar had probably climbed into the opening on the roof. He crawled through the ducts. Then the burglar kicked out the duct cover and dropped to the floor of the office.

When the burglar was ready to leave the store, he dragged the desk underneath the opening in the office ceiling. The burglar climbed onto the desk and into the duct. Then he crawled through the duct to the roof.

But who was this person?

POLICE BELIEVED that the burglar had climbed through a heating duct above the ceiling to get into and out of the building.

Fingerprint Processing 101

	Kind of Fingerprint	Can You See Them?
	Patent prints	These prints are clearly visible.
	Latent prints on hard surfaces	These prints are usually invisible to the naked eye.
	Latent prints on soft surfaces	These prints are mostly invisible to the naked eye.
	Impressed prints	These prints are visible.
	Partial prints	These prints are sometimes visible. It depends on whether they are patent, impressed, or latent.

Fingerprints can be found on different types of surfaces. So specialists use different methods to process them.

Description	How They're Processed
These prints are made by touching something like paint or blood and then touching other surfaces.	Patent prints are photographed.
These prints are formed by touching hard surfaces such as glass, plastic, or metal. The oil or sweat from the skin leaves a print.	Super Glue fuming, lasers, and dusting can detect latent prints on hard surfaces. For Super Glue fuming, an object that might have a print is put in a small chamber. Fumes from heated Super Glue are released into the chamber. A chemical in the fumes sticks to the oil and traces of sweat. When the fumes dry, the fingerprint becomes easier to see.
These prints are formed by touching soft or absorbent surfaces such as paper, cardboard, or unfinished wood.	Latent prints on soft surfaces can be detected with a chemical called Ninhydrin. Ninhydrin turns dark blue or purple when it comes into contact with traces of sweat from fingerprints.
These prints are made by touching something like gum that leaves a clear impression of the prints.	Impressed prints are photographed. And investigators can sometimes make a mold of them.
Partials are incomplete prints. They can be patent, latent, or impressed prints.	Software called "recognition technology" can read some partial prints. It can make identifications from incomplete data.

3

Expanding the Hunt

Desperate for clues, investigators move the search outside.

The investigators had figured out how the burglar had most likely broken into the store. They sent the fingerprint specialists to dust the heating system and the duct cover.

But they couldn't find any suspicious prints there either. The police expanded the hunt to the area around the building.

An officer went to the back of the building to

investigate how the burglar had gotten onto and off of the roof. The officer found a ladder near the building.

He also noticed something unusual. Next to the ladder, there were several wads of black tape.

The officer picked one up and noticed a print pressed into the sticky part of the tape. He carefully bagged the tape as evidence. He sent it to the crime lab.

Would the tape help the police catch the burglar?

WADS OF TAPE like this one were found behind the store. Investigators hoped that prints left on the tape would help identify the burglar.

4

A Hidden Clue

Did the burglar leave some evidence on tape?

Back at the crime lab, fingerprint specialist Oakley McKinney examined the wads of tape that had been found near the ladder behind the drugstore. "There were seven or eight pieces of tape," he says. "Some were wadded up or smashed. But I found three pieces with clear fingerprints."

McKinney focused on the three pieces of tape with clear prints. He put them on a table and shined bright light on them. Then he photographed the tape. He examined the photos with a magnifying glass. Bingo! McKinney had a good print to use as evidence.

"I was pretty excited," says McKinney. "Especially since there were no other prints at the scene. This could be the evidence the police needed to make an arrest."

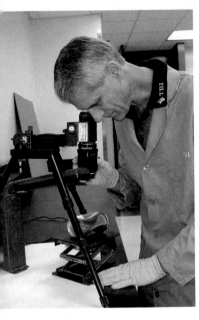

OAKLEY McKINNEY, a fingerprint expert, found a clear print on the tape left at the crime scene. Here he examines evidence from another crime.

Data Diving

McKinney scanned the photos of the fingerprints into a computer database that stores the prints of arrested suspects. Would the police be able to match the burglar's fingerprints with a suspect in the database?

Matchmaker

IAFIS helps police match perps to fingerprints.

Fingerprint specialists rely on the Integrated Automated Fingerprint Identification System (IAFIS, pronounced eye-AY-fiss) to help them match fingerprints.

IAFIS is a computer database that stores the prints of suspects who've been arrested. Fingerprint specialists enter prints they've found at crime scenes into IAFIS. Then the database searches through millions of prints from all over the United States. If it finds a match, the specialist checks to make sure IAFIS is right.

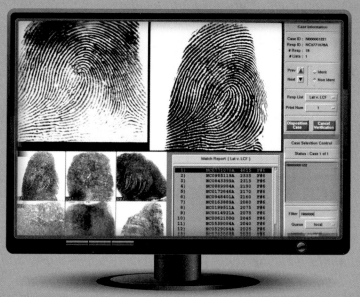

There are three types of fingerprint patterns: **loops**, **whorls**, and **arches**. Read on to see what type of fingerprints you have.

Loops are the most common type of fingerprint. About **65%** of fingerprints are loops.

In loop fingerprints, the ridges form loops, one inside the other. See how the ridges roll up and back down? That's the loop.

This is a **RADIAL LOOP** on the thumb of someone's left hand. On a person's left hand, radial loops point toward the left. On a person's right hand, the loops point toward the right.

This is an **ULNAR LOOP** on the thumb of someone's left hand. Ulnar loops are the opposite of radial loops. They point to the right on the left hand and to the left on the right hand.

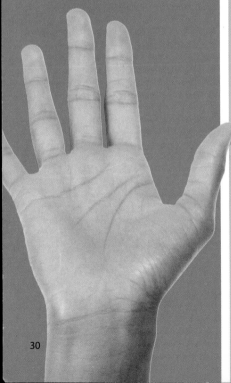

About **30%** of fingerprints are **whorls**.

Here the loops form a swirling pattern called a whorl. As you can see, the ridges are in the shape of a circle.

This is a **CENTRAL POCKET LOOP WHORL**. It has a loop and a whorl right in the center.

The **DOUBLE LOOP WHORL** has two loops.

This is an **ACCIDENTAL WHORL**. There's a whorl in the center.

Arches are pretty rare. Only about **5%** of fingerprints are **arches**.

In arch fingerprints, the ridges form a single bump or wave. The ridges move up to form a little arch.

This is a **TENTED ARCH** fingerprint. The arch makes a tent shape.

Sticky Fingers

The prints have a match—
but where is the perp?

Oakley McKinney returned to the crime lab. He ran the prints from the tape through the fingerprint database. It came up with a match. McKinney double-checked the computer's results. It was a hit!

"The suspect's name was Jeffrey Snyder," says McKinney. "He lived north of town. He had a prior arrest for burglary."

The police went to Snyder's home. When Snyder

LIKE SNYDER, this suspect tries to climb out a window after the police tracked him down.

saw the police, he tried to escape out a back window. But police officers tackled him in his backyard. The police searched Snyder's house and found some of the drugs that had been stolen from Gooch Pharmacy.

Prints on Tape

Snyder eventually confessed that he had stolen money and drugs from the store. He explained that he had put tape around the ends of his fingers. That way, he said, he wouldn't leave any fingerprints.

But then he made a mistake. He removed the tape and threw it on the ground behind the store. He didn't realize that his fingerprints were stuck to the tape.

That mistake made the burglary charges stick! ✘

The Man With No Prints

One criminal was willing to go to extremes to avoid leaving prints.

Robert Philipps, aka Robert James Pitts, had a long history of arrests. He was tired of getting caught. In 1941 he thought of a plan. He hoped it would keep him out of jail forever.

Philipps found a doctor who was willing to perform a strange operation. The doctor removed the top layers of skin on Philipps's fingertips. Then he replaced them with skin from Philipps's chest.

The plan was only partly successful. Philipps's fingerprints were gone. But the skin from his chest wouldn't grow on his fingertips. Instead, thick scar tissue grew on his fingers. He had no sense of touch.

The operation didn't keep Philipps out of jail, either. About six months later, he was arrested again. Police were surprised to find that their suspect had no fingerprints. But they took prints off the middle sections of his fingers. They compared the prints to files from the FBI, and Philipps was identified.

Something's Afoot!

Could *toe* prints trip up a criminal?

Like your fingerprints, your toe prints are one of a kind. William Gourley learned that the hard way. In 1952, he was found guilty of trying to rob a bakery. The evidence? He had left a print of his left big toe at the scene.

The ridges on the soles of your feet, the palms of your hands, and even the middle sections of your fingers also form unique patterns. So think of your hands and feet as permanent ID cards.

FILES

Handyman

Fingerprint expert Oakley McKinney helped catch criminals for a living.

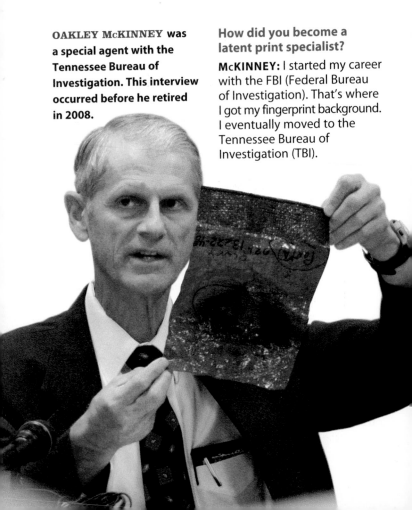

OAKLEY McKINNEY was a special agent with the Tennessee Bureau of Investigation. This interview occurred before he retired in 2008.

How did you become a latent print specialist?

McKINNEY: I started my career with the FBI (Federal Bureau of Investigation). That's where I got my fingerprint background. I eventually moved to the Tennessee Bureau of Investigation (TBI).

How does someone become a print expert?

McKINNEY: Every law enforcement agency has different requirements. The TBI takes recent college graduates. They train for two years. We require that they have 24 hours of chemistry during college. And ideally, we'd like someone who studied forensics [scientific techniques used to solve crimes].

What's your typical day like?

McKINNEY: My day varies greatly. Here, someone is always on call to go out to a crime scene. But most days I'm in the lab. I work on 25 to 30 cases at a time. Each one is at a different point in the investigation. On some cases, I'm waiting for photos. On others, I'm comparing photos and prints. I'm entering the prints into IAFIS on other cases.

How is your job different from the crime scene investigators we see on TV?

McKINNEY: On TV you'll see forensic specialists interviewing witnesses or suspects. That's pretty hokey. Our job is to collect, preserve, and examine the physical evidence that's left behind.

What kinds of cases do fingerprint specialists work on?

McKINNEY: Most cases overall are burglaries, but we work every crime—murder, rape, forgery, anything where a latent print is available.

What do you like about your work?

McKINNEY: I like figuring stuff out. I like working until I find and process a good print. It's kind of like a puzzle. And I like being part of a team that catches bad guys.

What do you dislike?

McKINNEY: To this day, I still don't like the blood and guts. But you just have to deal with it. You have to focus and be a professional and do your job.

Dusted and Busted

Here's some of the equipment that experts use to process fingerprints.

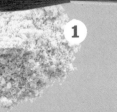

1 Powder and Brush: Dusting is the most common way to find prints, so print specialists can't live without powder and a brush.

2 Ninhydrin: This chemical is used to process fingerprints on soft, absorbent surfaces like paper and clothing. The chemical reacts to acids from sweat, making prints show up. Ninhydrin can even develop prints that were left decades ago.

3 IAFIS: This computer database can automatically search through millions of fingerprints. It helps law enforcers find the identity of criminals.

4 Fingerprint ID Card: These cards are used to record prints.

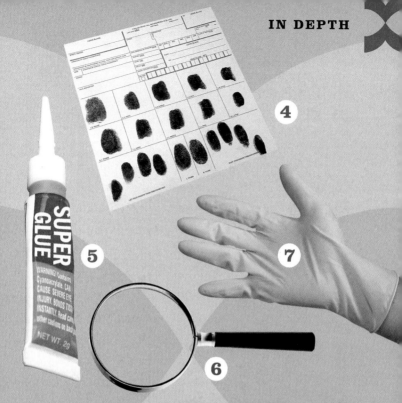

5 Super Glue:
Fumes from Super Glue make latent prints visible so they can be photographed. "Super Glue is one of the most valuable tools we have," says print specialist Oakley McKinney.

6 Magnifier:
A magnifying glass is a print expert's best friend. Zooming in on the print helps the examiner find all of its unique details.

7 Gloves:
Fingerprint experts usually wear gloves. Why? They don't want to mix their own fingerprints with the criminal's.

Can you match the partial print in the left-hand column to its full print to the right?

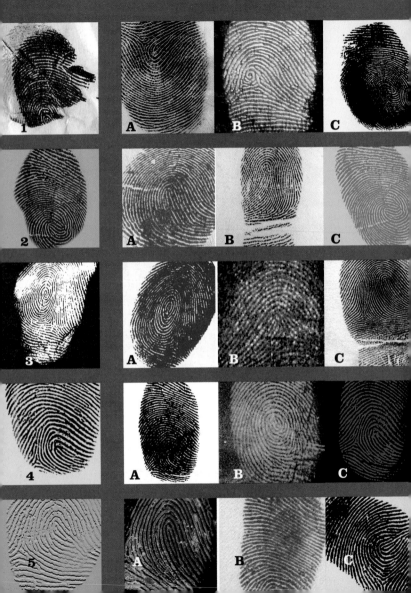

Evidence at Hand

Think you have what it takes to be a fingerprint specialist? See whether you can ID the prints on this chart.

Did you know that you leave a mark almost everywhere you go?

Take a look at the ends of your fingers. You'll see small ridges made of skin. These ridges have a purpose. They help you get a better grip on things you pick up.

These ridges form patterns called finger-prints. Your fingerprints were formed even before you were born. They never change. And no one has fingerprints just like yours.

How good are you at ID'ing prints? Look at each partial fingerprint on the left. Then choose the matching fingerprint from the four to the right.

ANSWERS: 1: C; 2: C; 3: A; 4: C; 5: C

43

Here's a selection of books and websites for more information about fingerprint analysis and forensic science.

What to Read Next

NONFICTION

Ballard, Carol. *At the Crime Scene! Collecting Clues and Evidence.* Berkeley Heights, NJ: Enslow Publishers, 2009.

Beres, D. B. *Dusted and Busted! The Science of Fingerprinting.* New York: Franklin Watts, 2007.

Beres, D. B. and Anna Prokos. *Crime Scene: True-Life Forensic Files.* New York: Scholastic, 2008.

Cooper, Christopher. *Forensic Science* (DK Eyewitness Books). New York: DK Publishing, 2008.

Hamilton, Sue. *Fingerprint Analysis: Hints from Prints.* Edina, MN: ABDO Publishing, 2008.

Mauro, Paul. *Prints and Impressions.* New York: Scholastic, 2003.

Owen, David. *Police Lab: How Forensic Science Tracks Down and Convicts Criminals.* Buffalo, NY: Firefly Books, 2002.

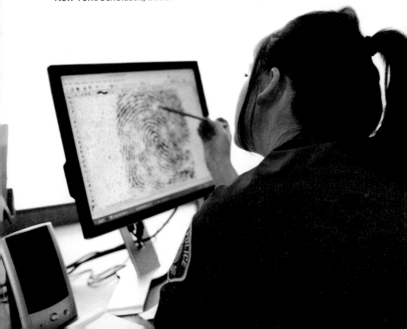

Platt, Richard. *Crime Scene: The Ultimate Guide to Forensic Science.* New York: DK Publishing, 2003.

Rainis, Kenneth G. *Fingerprints: Crime-Solving Science Experiments.* Berkeley Heights, NJ: Enslow Publishers, 2006.

Stefoff, Rebecca. *Crime Labs* (Forensic Science Investigated). New York: Benchmark Books, 2010.

FICTION

Brown, Jeremy. *Body of Evidence* (Four-Minute Forensic Mysteries). New York: Scholastic, 2006.

Conrad, Hy. *Almost Perfect Crimes: Mini-Mysteries for You to Solve.* New York: Sterling, 1995.

Websites

CSI: The Experience: Web Adventures
http://forensics.rice.edu

This site is part of an exhibit that has traveled to science museums around the country. It immerses you in hands-on science while leading you through the challenge of solving a crime mystery.

FBI Kids' Page
www.fbi.gov/ fun-games/kids/kids

Here you'll learn how the FBI conducts investigations.

Fingerprint Dictionary
www.fprints.nwlean.net

This site features a long list of terms used by fingerprint experts.

Forensic Science
http://library.thinkquest. org/04oct/00206

This site provides an in-depth look at what happens at a crime scene and how an investigation works.

Young Forensic Scientists Forum
www2.aafs.org/yfsf

This site is part of the American Academy of Forensic Sciences. It has all kinds of information about the field of forensics and ways to get involved.

GLOSSARY

absorbent (ab-ZOR-buhnt) *adjective* able to soak up water or other liquids

aka (AY-KAY-AY) *abbreviation* short for "also known as"

analyze (AN-uh-lize) *verb* to examine something carefully in order to understand it

arch (ARCH) *noun* a fingerprint pattern that is made up of a single raised bump or wave

database (DAY-tuh-bayss) *noun* a collection of information stored in a computer

duct (DUHKT) *noun* a passage that allows air to move through a building

dust (DUST) *verb* to brush with a powder to reveal hidden fingerprints

evidence (EV-uh-duhnss) *noun* materials gathered in an investigation to help prove someone's guilt or innocence

expert (EK-spurt) *noun* someone who knows a lot about a particular subject

FBI (EFF-BEE-EYE) *noun* the U.S. government agency that investigates major crimes; *FBI* stands for "Federal Bureau of Investigation"

fingerprint (FIN-gur-print) *noun* the pattern of skin ridges on a person's fingertip

forensics (for-EN-ziks) *noun* the scientific tests or techniques used to investigate or solve crimes

forgery (FOR-jur-ee) *noun* a fake or copied document, signature, or work of art

fuming (FEW-ming) *verb* in forensics, spraying prints with a glue that has been turned into gas in order to make the prints visible

hit (HIT) *noun* a match; a hit on IAFIS means the computer has found a match

identify (eye-DEN-tuh-fye) *verb* to recognize or figure out what something is or who someone is

impressed print (im-PREST PRINT) *noun* a fingerprint left on a soft, flexible surface, such as clay or gum

latent print (LAY-tuhnt PRINT) *noun* a fingerprint that can't be seen with the naked eye

law enforcement agency (LAW en-FORSS-muhnt AY-jin-see) *noun* a government agency responsible for ensuring obedience to the laws, such as local police, state police, or the FBI

lift (LIFT) *verb* to pick up a fingerprint with sticky tape

loop (LOOP) *noun* a fingerprint pattern in which the ridges form a series of half-circles, one inside the other

Ninhydrin (NIN-hy-drihn) *noun* a chemical used to reveal latent fingerprints left on soft, absorbent surfaces like paper and clothing

partial print (PAR-shul PRINT) *noun* an incomplete fingerprint

patent print (PAT-uhnt PRINT) *noun* a print that is clearly visible; it's made when a person touches something like paint or blood and then touches another surface

perp (PURP) *noun* slang for "perpetrator," a person who commits a crime

process (PROH-sess) *verb* to gather information (such as fingerprint evidence) at a crime scene

print (PRINT) *noun* short for "fingerprint"

ridges (RI-jez) *noun* raised lines on the tips of your fingers that form the patterns of your fingerprints

scar tissue (SKAR TISH-oo) *noun* thick, dense skin tissue that sometimes forms as a wound heals

specialist (SPEH-shul-ist) *noun* someone who knows a lot about a particular subject

suspect (SUS-pekt) *noun* a person whom the police think might be guilty of a crime

whorl (WIRL) *noun* a fingerprint pattern in which the ridges form a series of circles, one inside the other

INDEX